Lighthouse of Dreams
Finding Light in Darkness

Lighthouse of Dreams

Teri Dourmashkin

Published by Teri Dourmashkin, 2024.

While every precaution has been taken in the preparation of this book, the publisher assumes no responsibility for errors or omissions, or for damages resulting from the use of the information contained herein.

LIGHTHOUSE OF DREAMS

First edition. June 18, 2024.

Copyright © 2024 Teri Dourmashkin.

ISBN: 979-8227705181

Written by Teri Dourmashkin.

To all those facing enormous struggles and feeling like there is no hope. This book is for you. May you find solace, strength, and a glimmer of light in these pages.

Banging and banging against the wall.
Feeling so frustrated, trains always stalled.
You're not to blame, circumstances insane.
Tearing my hair out, metaphors call my name.
My head is hurting, I don't want sympathy.
I'll close my eyes and dream of deep seas.

Feeling so sad washed away on a shore.
Carrots are dangling, I want more.
The pressure is intense, my heart wants to soar.
Black veil of tears, stop the torrents of rain.
Please do not feel sad for all of my pain.
Verses expressed an art, not in vain.

\.*~♡~*./

I speak to my Divinity every night and day.
My anxieties sky high, she whisks them away.
Is she real or has my subconscious gone astray?
I long for her lighthouse, help me find the way.
Soft whispers echo, "You will heal and find love."
I pray this is true, thank the heavens above.

TERI DOURMASHKIN

Pain that runs deep, burrowed holes in the snow.
From the top of my head to the tips of my toes.
My brain went amok, seeing monsters that glow.
It thinks I am in danger, or so I've been told.
I live amongst angst; I need a new home.
For every new season, faith finds a new zone.

\.*~♡~*./

Tearless tears, stuck in fear.
Cannot even swallow, choking on years.
My words seem trite, can't get them out right.
I want to express but feel like a mess.
Wells of sorrow drip down my chest.
Can't feel their wetness, they deceive me at best.
I hope and I pray, I am able to rest.

\.*~♡~*./

Sounds of anxiety rings in my ears.
Makes me go haywire, stay calm restless tears.
Turns my insides out, I shake, and I quake.
All day long, well into the night.
They are not of my own, such a perilous fright.
Give some peace, may my wings take flight.

I need to feel the touch of your skin.
I need old books tattered; new chapters begin.
I need to breath without gasping for air.
I need the warmth of your love and your care.
I need you to come to me, please let me fly.
I need solace and peace; I need to cry.

Let me lie on your chest fingers in my hair.
Let me cry softly, kisses in a tear.
Let me ask for your love ever so near.
Let me sob and sob, never stop for a year.
Let me unleash my torment, rivers that heal.
Let me feel safe in your arms, let me feel real.

Tears of frustration pelt in my heart.
I know you love me, but worlds apart.
If you could, you would be right here.
That I don't doubt, dark shadows that leer.
Too many obstacles piercing my soul.
Feeling such sadness, head needs to clear.
Climbing up mountains, feeling so cold.

Tears stuck like glue, trickling in my heart.
Need to run away, make a fresh start.
Trapped within walls made of old salt.
Head is aching, is it somebody's fault?
I climb, I struggle, I persevere.
Is anybody listening, my words are severe.
I can't be concerned; my voice must be clear.

Depression sneaks in a thief in the night.
Sun morphs into blackness, can't see the light.
Skies tinged with gray, flowers decayed.
Feelings are sinking, feeling betrayed.
Can't seem to shake it, empty holes on display.
Just sit and be with it, pray it passes this day.
Be kind to those who can't find their way.

Why so much worry, why so much dread?
Monsters crawling under our beds.
Brains spinning and spinning eyes turning red.
Why do we do this, stress pounding our heads?
Take a deep breath, anxiety will shed.
Always miracles, allow them to spread.

Every day a new beginning, a promised dawn.
Things so predictable, grey tinged storms.
But sometimes in an instant, magic appears.
It takes you by surprise, shedding all despair.
Hang onto this hope because it is real.
Just have faith, believe, just feel.

Please tell me the future, let me just rest.
Life is so curvy, twisting roads, hanging vines.
Let go of the anxiety, try to accept.
Believe in yourself, a world that is kind.
To genuinely love is a gift so divine.

\.*~♡~*./

Sadness sweeps over me, a gentle rain.
Wish it would cleanse me of all of my pain.
Physical, emotional, it's usually the same.
Emotions sing songs that call out your name.
If dormant and buried, you'll feel the sting.
Such a deafening sound, the loudest of rings.
Open your heart, love the tears that you bring.

TERI DOURMASHKIN

Every now and then love comes along.
It pierces your heart, wash away all the storms.
When your beloved wants to crawl into your pain,
And feel it with you, a bond so sacred is born.
Tears that flow, pristine crystalline rain.
Unconditional love to the depth of our souls.
Mountains of obstacles, faith will console.

I feel as if time is slipping away.
Running through my fingertips, lost in a haze.
Anxiety streaming, ominous rivers betray.
Please let me see into the future,
Doesn't work that way.
Faith that is waning, need brighter days.
My pain an alarm screaming,
Hold on, magical sleighs.

Excruciating pain, monsters in the night.
Robs you of your dignity, your entire life.
My sweet sister Deb is in such a fight.
My heart is with her, such a terrible fright.
Putting on a smile is just a facade.
Underneath it all, just stabbing that robs.
Where did she go, her beautiful old self?
She is still there, but her body says "no."
Invisible to others yet sears into her soul.
A torture chamber, breathe fire and cold.
Lying in bed, tears crimson red.
So weary, exhausted, so filled with dread.
Pray for her now, this angel needs rest.
Wrap her in warm blankets, please no more tests.

A love as pure as crystalline snow.
Someone who loves you the more you expose.
Vulnerabilities dig down into black holes.
Unconditional acceptance I have never felt.
Until now, my heart truly melts.
Tears trickle into my heart and soul.
Sacred treasures to surely behold.

If we could hand out love in our hands.
If we could spread kindness, you'd understand.
If we could sweep out cruelty and hate.
If we could feed every hungry child, no debate.
If we could see the goodness of every heart.
If we can convince one another,
It's there from the start.

\\.*~♡~*./

He is sweet, he is light.
Everything I've wanted, dance into the night.
So remarkably close, yet so far away.
I want to kiss you this very day.
My dreams are few, simplicity is due.
I want to heal and hold you too.

TERI DOURMASHKIN

Beauty is only skin deep.
From the top of our heads to the tips of our feet.
Wrapped in new bodies fell back to earth.
With each new incarnation, sunrise, a new birth.
We must take care of it, treasure its worth.
But the heart is the most beautiful,
Fall in love with that first.

Underappreciated, unacknowledged, it hurts.
Fly away little hummingbird, believe in your worth.
Some like to jab, incompatibility gone awry.
I sit in my pain, just let me cry.
Tears that don't come but felt in my heart.
Help me believe, I will make a clean start.

Depression sinks you into a dark hole.
Happiness not promised, nights so cold.
So ubiquitous, days are unknown.
So many suffer, tears all alone.
Light turns black, no shades of gray.
Trudging on snow caps, dreary winters day.
Have compassion, wrap your arms out today.

Toxic fumes are making me weak.
Not from the air, but from a person I speak.
One minute loving then screams in my ears.
Complications make it hard to bear.
My words just need to be put on the page.
No empathy, no judgment, I will find my way.

I hear sobbing and sobbing, hurting my ears.
Should I still have compassion, after so many years?
Millions of apologies, empty cesspools.
I am not an ice queen, loveless and cruel.
Am I losing my mind, I feel like I am?
I need to find faith, it's in my own hands.

\.*~♡~*./

If I could gaze into your eyes,
It would bring me such solace, no more rivers that cry.
Cast the past behind me, closing torturous doors.
On nights, I struggle, I crawl on the floor.
You help pick me up, your spirit I adore.
The more darkness I hand you, you love me more.

I sit and stare out the window and gaze.
Sometimes my mind is in such a haze.
I want to have fun, go out and be free.
Sing silly songs and dance with such glee.
Where did my life go, lost among hidden trees?
There must be a reason this is happening to me.
Help me out of the darkness into the light.
Help me not to suffer, let it all be all right.

\.*~♡~*./

My strength is my savior, but I'm human you see.
I must stand proud, a strong victory.
Come and hold me until daylight.
Kiss my forehead, my eyes till midnight.
Wash away my fears, let's dream through the night.
Please come to me when I am asleep.
Be with me in spirit when I silently weep.
I need you, I want you, we were meant to be.
Think of me on this new day, love's not a mystery.

\.*~♡~*./

My poetry my savior, my lighthouse to life.
Verses that speak of joy and such strife.
I must be true to my heart and soul.
Words not to impress that's not my goal.
Neither do they ask for empathy.
These gestures are kind, but this is my art.
Verses that flow right from the start.

Sometimes you have to wait for true love.
Do not give up faith, sweet hummingbirds.
You'll know when it's real, it sings to your soul.
If your hearts touch before your very first kiss,
Just know that it's magic, never dismiss.
Patience and faith move mountains pure bliss.

TERI DOURMASHKIN

I live in my dreams, sweet little tricks.
Your thoughts are powerful, dancing in air.
The Universe takes what you feed it.
Spoons it back with no flare.
It is not personal, so please beware.
Nourish it with riches, love, and great care.

You are so many miles away.
I cannot wait to hold you someday.
Your love velvet chocolate I fly to the moon.
You are my soulmate, my lover, I swoon.
I fall into pieces on the floor,
You pick them up gently, feel it down to my core.
Eyes silky blue, it's you I adore.

TERI DOURMASHKIN

Traveling through lifetimes, dark images, I weep.
Thrown off a sea cliff, my soul left this earth.
An Indian Princess killed in her sleep.
My fear of heights, I need a rebirth.
Sleeping alone, I need solace so deep.
A tapestry woven thousands of years.
I stand here today, still fighting these fears.

I close my eyes, squirming out of my cocoon.
It's tight, it's painful living in this womb.
As I come out, I suffer dark wounds.
Physical and emotional, rebirth on the moon.
I flutter my wings, so bold and so bright.
I fly away, shedding all of my frights.

\.*~♡~*./

I feel stuck in between two different worlds.
One with torn pages, the other lustrous pearls.
I sit and I wait, no crystal balls.
My love he does wait, so tender and sweet.
He walks with me in darkness, forever to keep.
I must hold on tight, symptoms a fright.
My faith I will find, dig deep in the night.

\.*~♡~*./

My stomach is sinking into my heart.
Pain is screaming emotions aloud.
Can be heard in the biggest of crowds.
A symphony of music that just won't depart.
Suppression, repression, they love to pretend.
All is not well, learn to heal once again.

TERI DOURMASHKIN

\.*~♡~*./

One day turns into another.
Mediocrity is the name of the game.
But sometimes in an instant,
A tap on your shoulder,
Turns the ordinary into a flame.
Believe in miracles, they call out your name.

\.*~♡~*./

I dream of your scent, after the rain.
Take my hand, cleanse me of my pain.
I wake up feeling frightened, I call out your name.
I wish you could hear me; I imagine it's true.
Tame my anxiety, hold me all night through.
I'll try to be patient, please think of me too.

Can you touch someone's soul before you've met?
The heart knows no boundaries,
Crash through physical depths.
Love an energy stronger than hate.
It soars through the Universe, no debate.
Just take the risk, it's never too late.

\.*~♡~*./

I dream of air that is pristine and clean.
I dream of our earth and its rebirth.
I dream of humans on the same team.
I dream of the day when there isn't a dearth.
I dream of the day when we realize our worth.

\.*~♡~*./

When evening comes, I float into your dreams.
You touch me, my scent melts into your flesh.
Love an aphrodisiac, lotus blossoms caress.
Passion is a flame words cannot express.
You know it, you feel it, hot lava streams.
Come taste my emotions, my soul is undressed.

Her name is Mina, such a beautiful soul.
She is my kindred spirit from centuries ago.
How do I know this? I just know it's true.
Her verses are a tapestry of so many hues.
Such a joy to write with her, we sit in the snow.
Sometimes cold and blustery, forever we grow.

Feeling so hurt, a punch in my heart.
Even people who love you can tear you apart.
I don't want empathy, just take in my words.
They jump on the page, they have their own urge.
Relationships fragile, porcelain doll on the floor.
Trust your intuition, it silently roars.

So much love from you beautiful souls.
Your words so profound, so gorgeously told.
My verses have touched you, for that I am blessed.
I sit in my chaos, sometimes feel like a mess.
You echo the beauty I share; you say it's a gift.
My heart is in tears, I am forever enriched.

There are things I long for I just can't touch.
At least not now, my heart is crushed.
Where is my faith, my divine given belief?
In so much pain, just need some relief.
We come here to learn, to grow and yes, hurt.
It's this thing called life, just cannot divert.

I kiss you; I love you; I look into your face.
We are just human; we both make mistakes.
We own them and apologize for such sweet loving grace.
You hold me in my darkest despair.
You crawl into my pain and sit with me there.
Our love is so sacred, nothing else to compare.

How many times do I need to pray?
I just need this pain to go away.
Feeling flooded, washed away rocky shores.
Life is a mystery, forbidden doors.
Peek behind thin gauzy veils.
Dare to ask, the answers are yours.

\.*~♡~*./

And in the darkest days of dawn,
A dark mist clouds my eyes, inky storms.
Everything turns to rust early morn.
Pain in my head makes it hard to think.
I need clean windows tinted pink.
Rose colored glasses I toast with a drink.

If the world could bathe in love and kindness,
We would transform the entire Universe.
Dip your toe in, just for a start.
Let it wash over you, let it melt your heart.

I drift in and out of a daze.
Floating on moments of joy, then dismay.
Life has a way of calling the shots.
Some circumstances run away spinning tops.
We do our best, that is all we can do.
Be kind to yourself, and let your love be renewed.

TERI DOURMASHKIN

Stomach in knots, twisted ropes on display.
Life is so complicated, pulls my heart every day.
Life gives us torrents and torrents of rain.
Is their meaning divine, some higher praise?
Suffering expands us and makes the heart grow.
After too many battles, I pray love just flows.

To all of your warriors slashing demons every day,
I give you my love, your strength does amaze.
Lying in bed, just want a rebirth.
Eyes search for an angel some snippets of peace.
You struggle, you scream splintering earth.
Hang onto that rope, your savior, your release.

We can only do the best we can do.
If you could have done better, you would have done so.
Accept where you're at, sans rabbits out of a hat.
Self-love is healing, please give yourself that.

\.*~♡~*./

Your words soothe me in my darkest despair.
You lift me up into rarefied air.
No matter what words slip off my tongue.
You love me even more; a new earth has begun.
It is pure and honest, raw tender care.
It is you who I want, I lay my soul bare.

TERI DOURMASHKIN

The greatest love songs pierce your soul.
They go very deep, you listen, they unfold.
They bring out desires, for beauty to be told.
Stories of longing, an aching uncontrolled.
Look into my eyes, please let me see.
Come show me your love, such ecstasy.

Some things just get harder to take.
I look up above and just ask for a break.
Feeling so weak, like a broken bird.
I know I am strong, but my voice isn't heard.
I clamor, I claw, get away from this pain.
Sometimes feel like I am going insane.
I have to find faith, bless me with that grace.

\.*~♡~*./

Not very often do we meet our true love.
So exceedingly rare, white sacred doves.
Relationships overfilled with plight.
So much blame, deaf ears in the night.
Tripping on each other hurts like a knife.
When you find real love, just let it flow.
Hold each other tightly, never let go.

Depression is sneaky, it steals your life.
Palettes of color so bold and so bright,
Fade into darkness, black shadows at night.
Feeling so tossed; eyes can't see the light.
The sharpest of blades crushes your dreams.
Have compassion for those lost in mid-stream.

\\.*~♡~*./

True love is worth the wait.
A treasure bestowed celestial gates.
Obstacles may sometimes be Divine fate.
If your heart says, "yes," embrace inner faith.
Hummingbirds dance around you with grace.
They'll bring your beloved, your forever soul mate.

Imagine a world where there's no hate.
Imagine a world where we all can relate.
Imagine a world where we admit our mistakes.
Imagine a world where love is not a debate.
Imagine a world where kindness prevails.
Imagine a world where acceptance is unveiled.

Love is so rare like a painted crimson sky.
Yet so many challenges, I could sit and cry.
Sometimes obstacles can teach, while others just hurt.
Tears in my heart, difficult to lay down a verse.
I don't want sympathy, just hear my voice.
Complex decisions, so hard to rejoice.

Even amongst the rubble, we must find some light.
Even if you're struggling, there are gifts within sight.
Gratitude will open your heart even more.
Find it under rocks, or under the floors.

\.*~♡~*./

Things can hurt, things can ache.
Can be physical or a heartbreak.
Dig deep within, buried caverns, no sin.
Your darkness is beauty, not delicate porcelain.
Shades of gray morph into light.
Take time to heal, it's your God given right.

\.*~♡~*./

True love is beautiful, red diamonds in my hair.
So rare and honest, a breath of fresh air.
Sometimes it's difficult, obstacles may scare.
Humans can move mountains, nary a care.
Your heart knows your soulmate, a magnet you share.
Believe in magic, it floats everywhere.

\.*~♡~*./

I walk through a mind field covered in frost.
My feet are bare, my mind is lost.
So much fear, don't know what this will cost.
One wrong move, I merge with the air.
I'd give up everything to swim with the bears.

Every once in a while, love comes along.
Makes your toes curl, makes you feel you belong.
Truth is the seeker, that weeds out deceit.
Some hurt you badly, little dolls do weep.
Yet the ones with the hearts so rare and true,
Will keep you in heaven, tender arms around you.

Nobody said life is fair.
You pray for the best,
Close your eyes, or just stare.
You can only do the best you can do.
Take a deep breath.
Love yourself, just choose you.

\.*~♡~*./

When you love another, you feel their pain.
Sitting under showers, such harsh pelting rain.
Whether friends or lovers, love is real, not a game.
You would do anything to ease their torment.
Just to quiet the suffering, even for one moment.

Authoring poems with a migraine, many times a week.
Do they make any sense do you take a little peek?
It's a big distraction, I fight with my might.
I need to create, run away from the fright.
I'll rest in a while; may angels soothe my head.
I melt into more struggles, then take refuge in my bed.

We fear so many things, made of dark woven cloth.
Much of it our own doing, in a daze feeling lost.
Anxiety runs amok, high wires, sad songs.
A viscous circle; turns gone so wrong.
There are no monsters under your bed.
Try to wake up and not feel the dread.

If I crawl into the recesses of my mind,
Will I be terrified, or will I find the Divine?
So many caverns to crawl in and find.
Often at opposites, different lenses at times.
Lightness and darkness merge in twilight.
Accept all there is, please give up the fight.

My dreams are of healing in broad daylight.
Please let me accept and give up the fight.
Crawling on floorboards can't catch my breath.
Dig into dark holes, mind boggling depth.
Been tossed around a torn ragged doll.
I hurt, I learn, I hear my name called.

Sometimes a union just doesn't work out.
Yet, there is still a love there, of that I don't doubt.
My heart is trembling, don't want him to hurt.
He has already walked through flames, scorched earth.
My heart is sinking, can't go through this again.
Can only wait, endless days begin.

Poetry is a piece of art.
Each reader will interpret via their heart.
Each sees through their own-colored lens.
Life's experiences mold, and they bend.
There is no right or wrong.
I put pen to paper, my verses my song.

TERI DOURMASHKIN

\.*~♡~*./

Crashing cars spin in my head.
All I want is some peace, stop the bend.
The strongest of the strong still need to mend.
Give me some space, give me some air.
My words are my art, I lay my soul bare.
Nothing to feel shame for, is that so rare.

Would you go to the ends of the earth for me?
Would you wrap me in love sacred mystery?
Would you embrace me so tenderly a child's touch?
Would you keep all your promises, never give up?
Would you take my heart into your hands?
Would you hold it carefully such soft linen sand?

Pain just banging in my head.
Emotions run deep, buried under my bed.
Monsters flicker then disappear.
They think they are clever, only to reappear.
Only an illusion of my brain,
She wants to scare me, maybe go insane.
My strength is my savior, won't play those games.

Your love for me melting chocolates so sweet.
Your soul enters mine, just swept off my feet.
A symphony of Mozart my heart skips a beat.
I need to feel safe, some solace, some peace.
Take my heart in your hands, forever to keep.

I wish I were a guru enlightened so bright.
I could tune out the pain, the anguish the fight.
I would dream of other worlds and float on the sea.
I could be whoever I wanted to be.
I could be on a yacht, hair flowing sweet breeze.
I deserve to be free, my body at ease.

Queens and Goddesses, you light up each day.
You've climbed rugged mountains, lost, and dismayed.
You still get the strength to pave your own way.
Your pains, your heartache, woven into your soul.
You are a fighter, so beautifully bold.
A sisterhood of slayers, hearts lined with gold.

TERI DOURMASHKIN

Love is the answer to the world's ills.
Dip deep in your heart, let it all spill.
Let it flow to those so alone.
Show them your kindness, let it be known.
Holding hands united we stand.
We are all God's children, wouldn't that be grand?

My dear friend's heart as beautiful as blue skies.
Her name stands for "love," there is no wonder why.
Her name is Mina, a poet of such grace.
Every word, every verse is yours to embrace.
Her soul is so wise, incredibly old.
Her imagination takes flight, soft silky gold.

Memories of a different life, another place.
Sometimes mere whispers a gaze at one's face.
Centuries tumble, lost in gossamer space.
Hand in hand, we traveled back to our home.
Everything so familiar, cloudy images erased.
So many lifetimes, two poets, never alone.

I am one with the Universe, echo bold words.
I set my intentions, let love winds be heard.
A heart that is tender, baby blankets divine.
Whispers in your dreams you feel my soul cry.
One with my heart love grows on a vine.
I long to be with you, forever through time.

Sadness grips me into my core.
Even people who love you can open old sores.
I don't want sympathy just want to be heard.
Just take in my words, fly away hummingbirds.
Love can bring both solace and pain.
You can dance in the moonlight or icy rain.

My emotions all jumbled, dancing with pain.
I wish I could sing in the pouring rain.
My heart is turned upside down.
Feel like a queen who's lost her crown.
Don't know what to think or what to feel.
Planes land in my stomach, not made of steel.

I am bold, I am fierce with feathered wings.
I am fragile, I am scared, I am all of these things.
My heart is as big as the ocean is wide.
My voice is as strong as the stormiest tides.
I am a woven tapestry never to hide.
I am who I am, I will take off and fly.

Dark sweeping tides roll out to sea.
Releasing a loved one tears a heart into three.
Words that pain me, can this really be?
Sadness that sits in the seat of my soul.
A tiny voice whispers, "It's time to let go."
Don't want to do it, clutching a rope.
Fading sunsets, fading hope.

Love can be complicated, a rubrics cube.
Some pieces splintered and fall down a tube.
Others so beautiful, like heaven on earth.
Your words of love such a tender rebirth.
No guarantees, fate takes its turns.
Miracles happen, just breathe, and discern.

In the silence of darkness, I reach for the stars.
I pray to the Gods, disappear naked nights.
Gasping for air, I choke on thick scars.
My body speaks to me, emotions held tight.
I need sustenance, nourished from Mars.
I just need some peace; I grasp for the light.

TERI DOURMASHKIN

\.*~♡~*./

I look into your eyes, soft baby blues.
Please take my hand, make my dreams come true.
We can move mountains just say it is so.
Tell me you believe this; it will make my heart glow.
Needing new chapters, we tear up old books.
We walk down quaint avenues, a brand-new outlook.

I vaguely remember memories lost times.
I ruled as a Queen with ice in her veins.
She was ruthless, not a jewel that was kind.
So, unlike me, unruly, untamed.
My mother's blood rolled into mine.
It was her unkindness never my flames.
She was not loved, forgiveness sublime.

\.*~♡~*./

I long to look into your eyes.
I long to embrace you, your skin against mine.
Hands so gentle, let me feel safe and sound.
Escaping high voltage, insensitivity abounds.
I want to weep into your chest.
I need this release, help me heal and rest.

You gaze at my eyes; your soul takes a spin.
Lost in such love, so much passion, not sin.
You draw me a bath by soft candlelight.
Flickers of tenderness so healing, so right.
You call me your Queen, such a delight.
Verses of poetry dance off your lips.
Just lean over and give me a kiss.

I don't need a mansion, or a big space.
Just want to feel safe wrapped in your grace.
Just you and me, we'll dance all night long.
Your skin against mine, such magical songs.
My heart etched deeply into your skin.
You feel it, you taste it, forever begins.

\\.*~♡~*./

I envision us together, every silky night.
May the Universe protect us,
Help us walk in the light.
Appearances not always what they seem.
Faith is the power to believe in our dreams.
Know it, trust it, let it go, let it beam.
Patience is everything,
Our lotus blossoms will sing.

I worry, I stumble across muddy shores.
So much is hurting, so much to endure.
Such a long journey, spikes dug in the ground.
I walk alongside hilltops, no relief to be found.
I weep in my heart, in my lungs, in my soul.
I long to heal before winter's cold.

I believe in jewels that seem out of reach.
So many lessons, so much to teach.
Faith is a measure of things the eyes cannot see.
You feel it, you know it, not a tangled mystery.
It will all happen, a miracle by the sea.

\.*~♡~*./

Butterflies flutter on my face.
Their beauty, their delicacy fills me with grace.
I want to fly on gossamer wings.
A sad concerto, black velvet lace.
Pain in my heart, it just wants to sing.
Release all the angst, let love embrace.
Freedom is near, I hear the bells ring.

You climbed into my darkest pain.
You felt it, you lived it, frozen pelts of rain.
Your love flows deep Mariana Trench.
You sip my mind can never be quenched.
Insatiable longings flames that ignite.
Fingers down my spine, I shiver this night.

TERI DOURMASHKIN

\.*~♡~*./

I want to heal like I breathe in the air.
Where to find joy when blinded by glare?
Memories of feeling free and at ease,
Now escapes me, just feels like a tease.
I close my eyes, imagine soft rain.
My body in comfort, sans any pain.
My verses my savior, hides the wet stains.

Crashing waves tickle my toes.
I look at the sun, endless tides of blue hope.
I close my eyes, let go of my woes.
I long for solace, let go of the rope.
Take my hand, tainted memories released.
I want to be with you, dip me in peace.
Your love a warm blanket forever to keep.

Meet me my love by the sand and the sea.
This is our dream, come comfort me.
I gaze at the horizon a tapestry of blues.
Just like your eyes, paint dipped in hues.
Gaze into mine, chocolate caramel in a kiss.
Let them enthrall you, taste what you missed.

As the stars lay down and go to sleep.
They still shine bright God's eternal peace.
They light up the world, a thousand-watt smile.
May your love do the same across the miles.
May you bring comfort to those in need,
Every act of kindness is so worthwhile.

There are angels who walk right here on earth.
You might not know it, but you'll feel their embrace.
They spread love freely,
They know your self-worth.
They'll wrap you in blankets of soft silky lace.
They'll hold your hand,
They'll give you, their grace.

He'll love me until the sky turns to stone.
He'll stay by my side; never alone.
He'll read me sweet poetry toes in the sand.
He'll take my pain while holding my hand.
He'll kiss my forehead, I melt, come undone.
He'll taste all my tears, we've only begun.

Things often feel rough.
Stormy seas crashing bluffs.
Hearts are in pain, let it be pouring rain.
Accept what you can turn around no man's land.
Barren and dry, wipe that tear from your eye.
Hands that are warm, dipped in soft velvet sand.
Kissed by night sky, it's your turn to fly.

He is heaven, he is earth.
He wants to free me from my pain.
Let the storm clouds fade, baby pink colored rain.
He feels my pain suffers a rebirth.
His head like daggers, his body hurts.
His soul is drenched into my core.
Please protect him, too much to endure.

TERI DOURMASHKIN

I feel your heartache deeply for mine.
Your love for me so pure for all time.
You'll take on my pain if it would erase mine.
A heart full of love sprouts mystical vines.
I don't want you to suffer, I don't want you to hurt.
Just be with me in spirit, when I fall into the dirt.
We've tumbled across many lifetimes before.
Reunited again, God's opened new doors.
That's why our bond is so very strong.
We journeyed through lives traveled roadways so long.
Sometimes struggles, many times sweet songs.
Come back into my arms, that's where you belong.

\.*~♡~*./

The lights have gone dim.
The sun has blown out.
Insides on fire, same place I have been.
Where do I land, whispers that shout?
I have no answers, can I still win?
I crawl back into the void filled with such doubt.

Feel like I can't do anything right.
Want to fly away but no end in sight.
Don't want sympathy, talk to my brain.
My words need expression, let out the pain.
If you find this too dismal, it is alright.
My verses my art, I put up a fight.
Some lives are difficult, walk on thin ice.

My stomach is on fire, where is the rain?
Stress pierces sharp arrows filled with such strife.
A day that's so long a dark winter's pain.
Please lift me up, erase all my plights.
It comes and it goes, the depth and the heights.
Release from suffering, I will bare it tonight.

TERI DOURMASHKIN

Sometimes you have to get lost in the dust.
Sometimes you have to regain trust.
Sometimes you have to take big risks.
Sometimes you have to let yourself hurt.
Sometimes you have to allow and revert.

\.*~♡~*./

Beauty is only skin deep.
Every woman is beautiful, angel kisses so sweet.
I don't care if she is 40 or 105.
Faces etched with lines, our joy, our pride.
Don't care if your breasts are small or large.
Doesn't mean anything, it's your heart that cries.
Stop body shaming, stop the lies.

I am beautiful, I am light.
I fought so many years, still in twilight.
There are no curses, no voodoo spells.
We crawl though heartaches ever new heights.
Not the enemy though it cuts like a knife.
Don't judge appearances often not right.
Just have faith, sleep peacefully tonight.

You make me shiver; you make me quake.
Your kindness, your tenderness such sexy black lace.
Attraction is what makes the heart ache.
It is the inside out such a passionate embrace.
To please me, to want me as your Queen.
That arouses me so fiery steam.

TERI DOURMASHKIN

I hear you whisper in my ear.
Melted chocolates divine, your soul so dear.
Such selfless prayers to take on my pain.
Don't want me alone in the frigid cold rain.
Never a love have I had before.
You've opened my heart like magical doors.

\.*~♡~*./

And in the darkness, I lay my head.
Such a fight, demons in my bed.
So much anxiety, I call to the Divine.
She's right by my side, loving and kind.
Words that calm, pain take a long ride.
I struggle, I trust, in the deity inside.

I look past the sky tumbling stars fall to earth.
I look to the Universe to seek wisdom, rebirth.
We are all one, often the game isn't fun.
We enter this life, so innocent, rising sun.
Weeds grow tall, some stumble and fall.
We are just human, let's break down those walls.

Your heart is sublime; your soul is so kind.
I bare my soul naked, my fears I unwind.
I share my dark secrets; they smolder at night.
You gently walk through them; you hold me tight.
You love all my scars, tattered and worn.
You are my beloved, kiss away all the thorns.

You lift me up when I feel so unwell.
Your spirit is with me, such soft tinkling bells.
So, understanding kisses yet to unfold.
Never to part, let us grow very old.
You drink in my auras like some magical spell.
Your light is so beautiful, pierces my soul.

Felling ill, stuck in quicksand.
I have a friend she gives me her hand.
I don't want empathy, that's not what I ask.
This is for her; my verses have been cast.
Her name is Mina, it stands for love.
She gives it to me, blue skies above.
She is a poetess, fly away sacred doves.

I am sunshine, I am dark.
I am joyous, I am utterly stark.
I am hopeful, I lose all my faith.
I feel trapped, a new beginning awaits.
I am contradictions light morphs into gray.
I am searing, no words left to say.
I pray to God for much better days.

I walk among shadows; I walk among dust.
The desert is barren, no mercy just rusts.
Then you came along purified the air.
I thank you for your tender sweet care.
I unleash my sorrows, all my despair.
You carry me in blankets, your love is so rare.

TERI DOURMASHKIN

I tip toe on fields emerald grasses that gleam.
Such jewels in my head, adorned like a Queen.
Riches, and extravagances slip through my head.
I just long for simplicity, peaceful nights in my bed.
I long to be with you, a safe haven of light.
Take my hand, lay with me each night.

I know a poetess so sweet and dear.
She comes to me when twilight is near.
We write our verses, inspiration with care.
Our hearts were bonded centuries ago.
We knew from an instant so much we shared.
Cobblestone streets, skies of indigo.

I stare at the dirt; I stare in the haze.
I need to be cleansed of this wicked pain.
Emotions scattered; my brain is not fazed.
Comes out of my hide am I going insane?
I try to feel them, the best I can.
I need an escape hatch; do you hear my name?

Don't miss out!

Visit the website below and you can sign up to receive emails whenever Teri Dourmashkin publishes a new book. There's no charge and no obligation.

https://books2read.com/r/B-A-QHNBB-VURMD

BOOKS 2 READ

Connecting independent readers to independent writers.

Did you love *Lighthouse of Dreams*? Then you should read *Beneath the Surface*[1] by Teri Dourmashkin!

[2]

"Beneath the Surface: A Poet's Reflection" is a stirring collection of poetry by Teri Dourmashkin, Ed.D., that delves deeply into the emotional and spiritual experiences of love, loss, and personal transformation.Each poem serves as a window into the poet's soul, offering reflections on life's profound moments and the inner journey of healing and rediscovery.Dourmashkin's work is characterized by its lyrical beauty, raw honesty, and the ability to touch the heart with its vulnerability.Through vivid imagery and passionate verse, **"Beneath the Surface"** explores the complexities of human relationships, the pain of heartbreak, and the courage needed to embrace new beginnings. This collection is an invitation to those who dare to explore their own

---

1. https://books2read.com/u/mvMNw6

2. https://books2read.com/u/mvMNw6

depths, to find understanding and solace in shared experiences, and to celebrate the resilience of the human spirit.Perfect for readers who seek poetry that is both reflective and inspiring, this book promises to be a compassionate companion on the path to personal renewal.

Read more at terilove.com.

About the Author

Dr. Teri Dourmashkin, Ed.D., is the founder of a minimalist skincare line, known for its natural ingredients and handcrafted batches. Alongside her skincare expertise, she is a passionate poet, blending beauty and wellness in both her professional and creative pursuits.terilove.com

Read more at terilove.com.